Kicking at Tombstones

Kicking at Tombstones

Kate Arnold

Black Eyes Publishing UK

Kicking at Tombstones
© Kate Arnold 2024

First published in 2024
Black Eyes Publishing UK
Gloucester
United Kingdom

www.blackeyespublishinguk.co.uk

ISBN: 978-1-913195-29-8

Kate Arnold has asserted her moral right under the Copyright, Designs and Patents Act, 1988, to be identified as the author of this work. All Rights reserved. No part of this publication may be reproduced, copied, stored in a retrieval system, or transmitted, in any form or by any means, without the prior written consent of the copyright holder, nor be otherwise circulated in any form of binding or cover other than that in which it is published and without a similar condition being imposed on the subsequent purchaser.

A CIP catalogue record for this title is available from the British Library.

Edited by:	Josephine Lay
Cover Art:	Photograph © Arnold family archive
Cover Design:	Jason Conway, The Daydream Academy www.thedaydreamacademy.com

This collection is dedicated
to all The Lovely Divers.

Kate Arnold is half of **Dead Anyway**

Dead Anyway
Vocals: Kate Arnold
Music: Marc Symonds

deadanyway.co.uk

Introduction

At the time of publication, I have written nearly eighty pieces for **Dead Anyway**, and it was important to me to choose ones for this collection which would work as poetry on the page. Some of the tracks which go down best at gigs, for example, feature an amount of repetition within the lyrics which might not make sense to someone who hasn't heard them performed live with the music.

The majority of these poems were written specifically for music which Marc has sent me, although *Iron Filings, Have You Gone?* and *Stay Sticky* started with my written piece which he then composed something around.

Contents

9   Introduction
17 The Receiver
19 Sonnets
21 Reptilian
27 Karma Schmarma
33 Whipping Boy
35 110%
41 Have You Gone?
42 Our Biology
44 The Now
46 The Lovely Divers
51 The Metaphor
52 Space Dust
57 Pigs in Blankets
65 Crocodiles
71 Pillow Heads
73 The Prowler
75 Conkers
79 Iron Filings
80 I Can't Stop Counting
82 The King and I
84 Indigo
89 Underbite
90 Stay Sticky
91 We Are The Rudderless
92 The Circulatory System
97 The Hollow

101 Thank You
103 Kate Arnold – Biography
105 How the poems came about
109 Full Quotes

The Receiver

original artwork © Andy Lewis

The Receiver

Your Disney eyes make mine spin shut.
My tongue is two fingers.
I know how to break the receiver.

Once I heard puppies, now my ears ooze mince.
You might as well talk to the mirror.
I know how to break the receiver.

This wouldn't work without you.
Your softness makes me hard.
I could rub your face in mess, but this is better.

I know how to break the receiver.

I have made the world from statues.
The heart is just a design.
And your denial is flies.

I am white noise behind a face of brick.
Read the graffiti, sweetie
and remember:

I know how to break the receiver.
I know how to break the receiver.

So why aren't you broken?

Even without a magnet in your hand
you draw the Blackbeard
as the Blackbeard is magnetically drawn to you.

Just look at your stupid face.

Truth is loud, fast and often.
Love is gone.
Go and ask your father.

I know how to break the receiver.

Sonnets

Cowardice has you complicit in this:
your upper lip bitten off as consent
and spat out into my parentheses.
I hold your silence to me, a present.

Kick away. You know you're out of your depth.
This Cyclops head, rumbling on your pillow
sees and hears all. You dream of horses' necks.
Little girl, what are you that you allow

red rags to be made from all you hold dear
and gored fast on the pitchfork of my tongue?
This bald lawlessness has stunned and pinned here
the voodoo doll of you, you have become.

Bathe, bathe again my sacred fontanelle:
you cry these dry black rhymes. You still won't tell

of events you will insist have occurred.
I construct our history from cuckoo clocks:
cuckoo clocks and tempers, heard and unheard.
Compliance is where your involvement stops.

You're no more than a finger down my throat
a poker into the brillo of ills
to rubberneck me from the antidote
you are. Yet I don't care. And you're here still:

tasered by the sound of your eyelashes
mercury plunging the length of your spine.
Kick away. My paparazzi flashes.
Little girl, such moments have made you mine.

Bathe, bathe again my sacred fontanelle:
you cry these dry black rhymes. And still won't tell.

Reptilian

These days are like tombstones you have to kick over
when you know you should be reading all the flowers.

But you're kicking at the tombstones
then you're kicking at the flowers
because you know damn well, don't you?

There's no one left to care but the thrown soldier bones
that rise up each night to fight you.

You start to smell petrol.

Reptilian. I am The Reptilian.

You've swallowed all the words in all the books
but you were really only panning for a code
that everyone else cracked but you never cracked
because you know damn well
don't you?

There is no password
there's no gypsy you've offended
and no almanac to look up this lack in either.

Your bellows are hacked.

Reptilian. I am The Reptilian.

So, the night creaks above you like a ship with no star
and my loaded tail flings you the swell
of what everyone else has that you should've had.

Except you know you can't have that, don't you?

Because you are the girl who sets the house on fire
time and time again, aren't you?

Aren't you?

You know damn well.
You were born the black lamb in a fallow field.
So how are you flat on this rack again
stuffed with a fuse again
my tongue fast in the base of your stem
yet again?

I'll fetch the matches, shall I?

This Tendency

original artwork © Andy Lewis

Karma Schmarma

Conscience is for the little people.
The long game is for losers.
I am immune to boomerangs.
Please stop pointing at mirrors.

I do not have to explain myself.
To you, or to anyone.
The truth is whatever got me what I wanted.
Yes, I am aware of roadkill.

Karma Schmarma. Tits and teeth. Pants on fire.

So what if there's a portrait up there?
I keep my new friends downstairs.
I talk like this now.
It comes with sucked money.

Hey, I sniffed hard for those cracks.
I dropped my soap by the door.
Do not underestimate my strap-on depression.
Remember my black tears?

Karma Schmarma. Tits and teeth. Pants on fire

OK, so there are skeletons in there.
I'll just hang this new dress elsewhere

and piss on history.

It was this or the knife
and your dignified silence came in useful.

Never say sorry, never say thank you.

I never say sorry.

My tits
my teeth
my pants

your fire.

Whipping Boy

original artwork © Andy Lewis

Whipping Boy

My heartthrob is the moon:
standing off, never dropping into that
magnetic well.

Eyes averted.
That yawn stage right
the truthful side.

No trick isosceles tip can magpie
my acid eye. No rubber ear presses
against these membranes.

You'll never see me swivel
for a fake dog whistle.
Clever dick. Whipping Boy.

Red rags, hypodermic words.
Electrodes in my cricket heels.
Titanium walls
a claustrophobia stampede.

Lid scratches.

There is something very wrong with me.

I am intravenously
off
key.

Inside me is a noise that sounds like dying.

There is something very wrong with me. Pussy foot. Clever dick.

Whipping Boy.

110%

Thanks for reaching out:
good to touch base offline.

Moving forwards
it's about a deep dive to push the envelope.
Can you ping me by COP? Awesome sauce!

So, peeps! Two more sleeps 'til
cheeky hollybobs with hubster & the fur babies.
#blessed
#my world.

Famalam.

Literally getting all my ducks in a row here
obviously.

But do you know what?
To be fair, at the end of the day it is what it is:
a game changer, no brainer, rollercoaster.
A whole raft of new normal.

Can we cover it off? Flesh it out?
Put a pin in it? Best practice.
Drill it down? Bottom it out?
Cascade it?
Bite the bullet.

Clear blue sky, bud.
A skinny jean, killer heels
a pop of colour: empowered.

Stunning, babes.

Nom nom.
Om nom nom.
Food baby.
Bless.

Shabby chic.

Heads up: link in bio
these bad boys are the next level!
110%.
Triggered?
Bantz.

Asking for a friend: am I being unreasonable?
I'll just leave this here.

You ok hun?

Uptick. Smashed it. Iconic.

I know, right?
(Mic drop)

Trip Switch Lips

original artwork © Suzanne Barrett

Have You Gone?

The sharp scratch of dawn
and it feels like you've gone.
Clouds fumble my eyelashes, jab the melting frame.

This morning smells of water.

Tiny strings that dangled you swing bloodied & vacant.
And yet, no fairy came.

Has the night ripped away my name
flung it to the ground, heeled it flat to just another word?
Am I now one more flower to escape you?

I was your daughter.
No matter.

My last job is to iron your debris:
the stump of your tongue tip
that shark's grin, the eyes a jackpot of wild mercury.
And to write this.

I steady again your drooping deadhead.
My scarecrow is being razed to the ground.

Our Biology

Something very wrong is strutting our streets.
360° headed, daddy long legged
drip, drip, dripping into our women.

Stretch it, sculpt it, erase it, shape it. Post it, share it.
Make it so and you're good to go.

The hot coals of childbirth
we're meant to pretend didn't happen.
Fuck the baby: how soon were you back in your jeans?
Size zero?

Put a stitch in for the husband.
Spanx it, tuck it, liposuck it. Post it, share it.
Make it so and you're good to go.

And don't get me started on the pubic hair deniers

or the poor weird-faced nannas:
pumped with plastic, frozen with poison
so no one can tell that they're really thinking.

Do you think anyone noticed I got old?

Peel it, inject it, plump it, smooth it. Post it, share it.
Make it so and you're good to go.

Well, *you're* good to go.

This is a broadcast on behalf of my face.
This is my straight to camera, and I will not be
taking questions.

Beware, beware.
I feel it in the hair on my chinny chin chin:
this is an ill wind.

Do not let it in.
Do not let it in.

Stub out the symptom. Starve the disease.
Give us back our biology.

The Now

I am the garden that backs on to your train.
Graffiti on a hoarding: sordid reading at close range.
Tights in the gutter.
Another shutter down forever.
I am bouquets at the side of the road.

Look for me in the tailback as you drive the flyover.
I am the wall of the underpass.
Everyone's eyes slide off me like egg.
At last.

I'm the dark sockets of a house with no power.
Trip switch lips.
Look for me in the now.

Have I broken into your heart yet?
Have I broken into your heart yet?

I'm talking in tongues again. I know, I know
but have I
broken into your heart yet?

Look for me in the trees at every roundabout you approach
in hot black rubber tracks.
I am nettles in the hedgerow.
A balloon, a blister pack.
I'm teething again but this time it's words, it's words.

Stand firm Kate.
I make a sweep of my face
and fake my forehead terror proof.[1]

This is not the time to step out into your headlights.
Look for me in the now.
This is not the time to step out into your headlights.
Look for me in the now.

It's in the words, the words, the words.
The words, the words, the words.

Look for me in the now.

---

[1] *Dante Alighieri, 'Hell, Canto XXI', in The Vision (Divina Commedia), trans. By H.F Cary (London: J.M Dent & Co, 1908) p90*

The Lovely Divers

All you lovely divers
where did you go?

You stole my whole globe for a helmet.
You strapped on your boots of lead
headed for a seabed that never spat you back.

And your criss-crosses blackballed me.
Your criss-crosses still blackball me.

All you lovely divers
are you swaying alone like Jesus scarecrows?
Or did you find each other?

Is it ok? Are you happy?
What's it like? Do you forgive me?
Is it the deliverance I promised you?

All the lovely divers
am I doing it right?
Are you proud of me?

It's just me on the boat now.

Are We Doing This?

original artwork © Suzanne Barrett

The Metaphor

Out here, the sky begins its syringe thing.
My albumen skull rides the horizon
a pendulum for an explanation.

Disused arms that flag
and wither.

I came out too early and now it's too late.
Are you getting the metaphor?

Thrust up through floorboards
to shiver a mistake
I'm constrained to make again
and again: are you getting the metaphor?

This pale hood shrouds a black anvil
my neck
never off an unseen block
couldn't hope to dangle.

I am nobody's business anymore;
a mangled spine that greens no summer.

I prod myself
as cattle.

Space Dust

A tennis ball in a sock against the garage door means
your sister's going to leave you alone for a change.

Phew.

Your dad's watching cricket in a roomful of smoke
curtains tight against the sun
which means you're not allowed in either.
But what you don't know is that it's because he's hung over.

All you know is, he's scary.

Your mum's singing Tammy Wynette in the kitchen
but something in her voice and the song is telling you
not to go in there
just yet.

There's a rattle of a magpie.
You don't know it's a magpie
it's just a bird you don't even really hear.

Holding *space dust* in your mouth
makes your tongue go sore
but you do it because you don't want anyone
to know it's there.

Pour some more.

You hold on tight to the rough hips of the tree because
you're balancing on an orange and red striped beach ball.

You admire your toes. You look like a circus girl.

It's Saturday and the sun's going to burst soon
but skin cancer hasn't been invented yet &
you've got six whole weeks before you have to go back.

You'll be in the circus by then.

You might marry Mickey Dolenz
or Pete Duel.

You've already got the hat.

Pigs in Blankets

photograph © Marc Symonds

Pigs in Blankets

I am far too fucking tired and far too fucking old
to be told what to do or what to say or how to be.

I do not need any further direction.

Look, if you get such a massive erection from sharing your
perceptions, I'm pleased for you, feel free.
Just take it to someone who needs it.

I am not a child.
This body of mine turned itself inside out like a fucking lily
to grow and push out another person
and that stuff is hardcore. I can tell you:
that shit changes you.

Why do I have to look like that didn't happen?

Don't tell me what I need to do
or how I might want to think about having some work done
if I don't want to get left on the shelf. Mate,
I'm a fucking piece of work already: my own life's work and
happy to be left in peace on my own shelf.

Thanks anyway.

These women who look like they never ever
pissed themselves laughing with friends
or cried for days at decisions

they were the only one brave enough to make:
I'm supposed to want to look like them?

Read my skinny lips [2]
cosmetic surgery doesn't make you look young
it just makes you look weird.

Cosmetic surgery doesn't make you look young
it just makes you look weird.

Cosmetic surgery doesn't make you look young
it just makes you look weird.

And all
the same.
I have raised my children.
I have paid my rent all my life.
No, I don't want a fucking medal and no one died
but please, I'm just a bit fucking tired now.

And remember I still get paid less
which is apparently just a thing we have to accept.

And childcare then
and parent care now
is still just *my* problem.

---

[2] *William Shakespeare, Macbeth, ed by Cedric Watts (Ware: Wordsworth Editions, 2000) 1.3.45*

And another thing:

these instructions we are given how not to get raped on our way home, right? How about *they* get instructions how not to rape us on *their* way home instead?

These instructions we are given how not to get spiked, right? How about *they* get instructions how not to spike *us* instead?

Ask for Angela my arse.

And these instructions we are given how not to get raped by a policeman, right?
How about *policemen* get instructions how not to rape us murder us, or take photos of us when we're dead and WhatsApp them to all their friends instead?

Don't wear that. Stay sober. Text when you get home.
Oh, on and on and on it goes. It's the biggest ism of all time. It's as big as the sky. It's so big we don't see it as we go about our daily lives remembering all the fucking birthdays, which fucking bin goes out when, check for fucking tissues in everyone's fucking pockets and always have a stamp and always have painkillers and always have change for the fucking waitress because no one fucking else will.

And then, the pigs in fucking blankets. It's endless.

Remember to forget your art: your free time now is for housework.

And if you must do your little drawings/write your
little lyrics when the hoovering is done
make sure there's no fall out.

Don't shout:
sing in a little girl's voice, or sing like you're having sex.
There is nothing in between.

Remember: keep the peace, be jolly, accept rudeness
as banter and don't be too fucking clever.
And be grateful: he never beat you, cheated on you,
or shot you and the kids because you earn more than he
does, did he?

And now I have to delete all my social media accounts
so I don't get trolled. Oh, do your worst, arseholes.

That's not real life. This is.

Yes, I'm batshit, we all are and this is why.

The pigs in fucking blankets.

Bye.

Crocodiles

photograph © Marc Symonds

Crocodiles

Last year, I went down into my tunnel, and I ranted
(amongst other things) about the pigs in blankets.
And what do you know?
Lo and behold.
Trip trap trip trap:
my very first troll.

This is what we get
should we dare to put a head up over the parapet.
And when we call bullshit
on this bullshit
it's because of our hormones
and not the bullshit.

What? I'm just talking.

And now we have yet another set of instructions:
this time how not to get murdered on our way home
by a policeman.

Or police*men*.
Because there are, suddenly, a hundredweight
under investigation. So,
not just one bad apple then?

And what's with so-called covid arrests at that vigil
but it was ok to go to the pub the next week
and watch football?

We can tweet about the injustice
speak in parliament about the injustice
rant in tunnels all we like about the injustice
but injustice, it seems, just isn't injustice

when it's just us.

Men are afraid that women will laugh at them.
Women are afraid that men will kill them.

What? Margaret Atwood talking, not me.

Oh, of course it's not all men.
Oh, of course it's not all men.
It's not all crocodiles either.

Measured comment from a rational woman
will always be drowned out by a shouting man.
Never smile at a crocodile. Although
crocodiles, quite frankly, are easier to predict.

Cheer up, love, it might never happen.

Look around you, mate: it *already is.*

Houdinis of Ennui

original artwork © *Sara Vielvoye*

Pillow Heads

The peel of dawn

and I am feeling primeval
medieval
as if something deep
has just been revealed

and the world
the world is listening:
muted, grave
and sooty.

That bad fairy
spitting at my christening:
I'm starting to think it was me
and I've been
sleeping
for a hundred years.

Where else could I have been?

A dead man's oak
shackled static to the moon
that shattered to Niagaras of leaf
or the swift smelling salt
of stone teddy bears?

Which is the dream?

I'm in the wrong face.

No, I'm not crying
these are lightbulbs on my cheeks.

No, I am not crying
these are the lightbulbs.

Pillow Heads
came for me at dawn,
drummed me to the scaffold of 'love'.

But you?
You kissed my tiptoes.
You just kissed my tiptoes.

These are the lightbulbs.

The Prowler

Your lullabies are chemical. They steer the dark alone
simmering a moon.
Your body bolted.
Yet you'll wake to my blaze.
I have set off the alarms again.
I like to watch you rush whitely to the window.

If you fear the answer
then don't ask the question.
If you fear the answer
then don't ask the question.

I think we've gone beyond peeping, don't you?

Your wet finger picked up my direction.
Sinned against, I fling your bins across the garden.
You think I can't see you behind that sentry
of dictionaries, jabbing at your keys.
Jabbing at your keys.
Jabbing away at your keys.

If you fear the answer
then don't ask the question.
If you fear the answer
then don't ask the question.

I am the digit in your wardrobe
winkle pickers in the curtain
the mad cat flattened from your hangers.

Are you sorry yet?
Are you sure you haven't made a mistake?

You said this is what you wanted.

Love, it's time you realised
the prowler, this prowler
is already inside.

I was always inside you.

Conkers

Everything about this is sepia.
November, four pm.
Feed yourself to yourself
through the eye of my needle.

If no one is around to hear a tree hit the ground
did it even make a sound?
And when the felling made no sound, did
it ever happen?

Their morning walk will never unearth
that fork we have pursued.
I have swallowed you whole
waxed shut my lips with dew.

And they can cut me down with their dawns
before I'll ever let them see
the rings, the rings.

Oh, the rings you have stirred into me.

Love is locked, like conkers.

Falling, the tree fills both hands
smears our love into the sky.

Kisses in whispers
fifty feet high.

Unspoken Word

photograph © *Arnold family archive*

Iron Filings

A scar unzips the sky to aluminium pigeons.

Hippy trees wail their sleeves
against clouds of concrete.

A distant train
that rattled her hills
still rattles your hills.

She is hands of candles,
back home to the embryo.
Finger holes in snow
your glance catches.

You must scrub your hands of your heart now.

She is a letter in a fire
the hush of hymns;

and you, iron filings
to the magnet of absence.

I Can't Stop Counting

1 2 3 4 5 6 7 8   1 2 3 4 5 6 7 8   1 2 3 4 5 6 7 8 9 10 11 12 13 14 15 16.   1 2 3 4 5 6 7 8   1 2 3 4 5 6 7 8
I can't stop counting. I can't stop counting. I can't stop counting. Never mind, listen: I drove past your place today and they've got a bloody dreamcatcher hanging in the kitchen window - who does that? Also, their curtains are nowhere near as nice as yours were: looks like they came from Asda. Dunelm at best. Anyway, I'll tell you the rest when I see you. I'll tell you what else when I see you.

Oh.

9 10 11 12 13 14 15 16.   9 10 11 12 17 19 22 I can't stop counting. I can't stop counting. Because if I stop counting 16 17 44 because if I stop counting 18 20 91 because if I stop counting, because if I stop counting. Anyway, must have missed you on Tuesday perhaps you were somewhere at the back? No matter - have to get used to being eyes for the both of us now. You know, pretty much everyone turned up, even Soft Perm Pam - she's still very glam. Poor old girl.

It was a really good turnout, you know.

9 4 31 2 6 22 The nights are really drawing in now, aren't they? Can't afford the heating on anyway - winter duvet first! Bedtimes are the worst, of course they are. No dodging

the void then - like when they empty the bottle bank, and that silence afterwards is well, frankly guttural.

It was all a bit of a blur if I'm honest, but I think I got through the eulogy ok. I really hope you like what I had to say. Was it ok? Was it ok? Well, you can tell me all about it when I see you. You can tell me all about it when I see you. You can tell me all about it when I see you. You can tell me all about it when I see you. You can tell me all about it when I see you. You can tell me all about it when I see you.

The King and I

I touched a bonfire in my living room.
Just part of a calf left now, and two shoes.

Today, the globe
stuck in my throat.

We're apping our faces into cartoons
scrolling for tech neck factory jujus
arrested for holding up a blank A4
as the gold
rolls through our cold homes.
But you know: Paddington.

We'd trample a field of poppies
if it meant we got a selfie in
a field of poppies.

You were the same age
but your last carriage took twenty-six hours.
Twenty-six hours: that's twice the queue
and no one gave you a blanket, did they?

Your royal wave was from the stretcher
they wouldn't let me follow.

And on your birthday, framed behind glass:
tiny brave obedient fish in a mask

while that bastard
blond, balloon suit partied
laughing hard behind raw pastry hands.

No standard. No broken wand.
No last post for you
who never once complained.

Just: 'Bless you, Kate.
Thank you. Goodbye.'

The King and I have nothing in common.

Indigo

I've always been difficult. I know this.
I am cranky, hard to anchor
and I won't be told.

But you made me slow down.
'Stop,' you said.
'Look up.'

You'd tied a bow around the moon
looped it through a tree
so, it would always be up there for me
and I could see both the wood
and the trees
and locate the safe places
I need to hibernate
and wake up golden
      and wake up golden.

October is falling now
already confetti
while you have stood sentry
and let me howl from the cliffs
that there is no one
no one who can help me with this.

Quietly
wheeling the scenery in
wheeling the scenery out.

I know this is unlucky.
I know this is too soon.
and I am far too superstitious
to risk unfettering the moon

but this is all I have left to thank you with.

Because you
need to know this:
I may be tarnished
but you have shown me
        moments of golden.

These days are indigo.
These days are indigo

but you have shown me
        moments of golden.

Partially Eaten by Animals

original artwork © Suzanne Barrett

Underbite

Home for days now. I live in the trees.
Frantic static behind the scenes.

The stale of a whale belly
I alone have clawed.

Sleeping beneath a wolf skin
the cold clock tick of my own thaw.

I can't remember what I'm waiting for anymore.

That sky a dead eyeball through the keyhole.
Sirens slit the street.
Someone's getting away I see.

If only it was me.
If only it was me.

I have no right to, but I do
I miss you.
I miss the girl I am when I'm with you.

Curl myself back into a fist.
Rebutton the underbite.

Stay Sticky

Love, your grass is dead whatever the side.

You let the rain.
You let the rain try.
You clock that socket in a sky
that used to bear a beach ball.

And your heart is the magpie
burnt to a crow.

You're unhappy there
and all you want is to get back.
But you're unhappy *there*
and all you want is to get back.

Who's going to tell you the moon's not black
on a hooded night like this
when you wonder:

what's the point in having all the answers
when nobody's heard of the question?

Sleep.
Our fingerprint sweeps Ribena cheeks.
Stay sticky with the memory.

And don't you dare come here.

We Are the Rudderless

You came from a place of love and purpose.
That place no longer exists.

Only we, the truly rudderless
understand the importance of this

when all you have left is your own breath.

We found you by the side of the road
a dusting of snow

partially eaten by animals.

You have reversed across yourself for the last time now.
My silver blanket looks good on you.

Tonight, there will be no new notifications.
You have one new message.

Come on, give me the keys.

Tomorrow, you will be the grateful person
another chastened bird for our murmuration.

We are The Rudderless.
You are one of us.

The Circulatory System

Tonight, all my taboos lie in puddles around the room.
You get used to stepping out of them.

I've been trying to re-learn biology lately:
the circulatory system.
And arteries carry blood away
but veins lead straight to the heart.

Arteries carry blood away
veins lead straight to the heart.

It always looked like a map to me.
Although my sense of direction is
famously substandard.
But I'm trying to learn. I'm trying to learn.

This is not about one thing.

Nothing is ever about one thing.

If I had to choose from all the streets I've never lived in
it'd probably still be the one just around the corner
and I'd lose my way trying to get there
as I lost my way trying to get there.

This is not about one thing.

And arteries carry blood away
but veins lead straight to the heart.

Arteries carry blood away
veins lead straight to the heart.

I don't really know what it is I'm trying to say here.
Maybe it'll all become clear one day.
Maybe it'll be too late by then.
Maybe that's the point.

Geography, biology:
they've always been a mystery to me but
arteries carry blood away,
veins lead straight to the heart.

Tonight, I can't stop thinking about
all the junctions I got wrong
and how nothing is ever about one thing

and how all I ever wanted
was to go straight to your heart.

Tough, Listen

original artwork © Sara Vielvoye

The Hollow

You're shaken awake
by the silence of a mausoleum
your heart see-through balloons against the ceiling.
You tug-of-war your tongue up from your guts.
Fling it to the floor.

It's no good to you anymore.

In terror, you shoot the mirror
to a monochrome kaleidoscope
because it's never shown you anywhere like
this before.

And you realise: incrementally
you've achieved the empty sleeve
flapping with a nameless fear.

Flapping with a nameless fear
in a wind tinged blood orange warm.
And that crackle of your temples burning
is the crackle of your temples burning.

From a coffin lid sky so matt black with desire
no fingernail could gouge a star:
far off, still
the sad drill of a used-to-be moon
you know can no longer reach you.

This is the Hollow.
Damn right it won't reach you.

A wolf
in hand shadow cartoon
throats your moon as a pill
throats your silly moon as a pill.

Run if you will. Run
if you insist.

Just mind the wire that flicks the switch
to uprooting tree boots
in a deadly pursuit.

But is it dead? Is it just withheld?

This is the Hollow.
Welcome to the Hollow.

This is the Hollow.
Welcome to the Hollow.

Thank You

We feel incredibly lucky to know some extremely talented artists who have contributed their work to our projects, some of their art is included in this book, and our thanks go to them. Please do check out their other works online.

Thanks to Mick, Ted and Martin for their testimonials.

We would also like to thank Peter and Josephine at Black Eyes; and the radio hosts, play listers and reviewers (who absolutely know who they are) for their generosity and support.

Kate and Marc.

Kate Arnold - Biography

photograph © Gail Something Else

Kate Arnold is a MA Creative and Critical Writing student at the University of Gloucestershire. She was tutored by poets Carol Ann Duffy and John Harvey at The Arvon Foundation's Unpublished Writer's residential course in 1987, and her poetry has appeared in *Slowdancer* and *Aurora* magazines.

Kate also writes prose and drama; her short story *The Magnets* was included in the London Independent Story Prize anthology in 2023, and an excerpt of her play *The Good*

Piano was performed at The Everyman Theatre in Cheltenham's New Writing Showcase.

This is her first published poetry collection.

How the poems came about

I've always liked poetry that lances the heart, but allows space for the reader's own interpretation. I don't want to be told what a poem is about. I want to work it out for myself. I like the intimacy of the process.

Studying the twentieth-century poets for 'A' level, I was completely seized by the need to do to other people what Plath, Larkin, Hughes and Auden were doing to me. That was when I started to write my own poetry, and I haven't stopped since. I had a few things published, but I didn't consider taking it much further: it's always been about the creation for me.

Later, when forming a band, I stuffed whatever I happened to be writing into the structure of songs; and while singing, playing and collaborating was fun to begin with, I found myself feeling increasingly infuriated and creatively claustrophobic. Perhaps I'm just not a team player; all I knew was that I was beginning to feel indignant at having to run what I was writing past anyone else - and that included an audience. So, when the band imploded, I was very happy to retire from performance and I went back to writing for myself.

Marc and I had always had close friends in common. My band supported his a few times, and I'd long been intrigued by his knack for devastating musical beauty juxtaposed with a bafflingly uncompromising stage stance. He approached me at a gig in 2019: he'd heard I wrote poetry and asked if I'd ever thought of recording some of it. Apparently—and I have no memory of this—I said, 'why the f**** would I want to do that?' I can only assume that what I actually meant is that I couldn't imagine why anyone would want to listen; and, of course, I had had wine. Luckily for me, I changed my mind within the hour: we met up four days later and started work on what turned out to be *The Receiver* EP.

Almost straight away, Covid hit; and, listening back to those early tracks on the *Kicking at Tombstones* compilation, I can hear the uncertainty and claustrophobia of that time. Marc was personally very affected by Covid, and there's a fragility in the music he wrote for me to contribute to. It reflected everybody's fear at the time: the empty streets, a disorientating lack of routine and that sudden, shocking awareness of mortality. Although I wasn't expressly writing about Covid, there's no doubt that what he was producing, mirrored the atmosphere I wanted for the words.

The idea of me singing was never discussed for Dead Anyway – I think we both understood that I wanted to return to my roots in poetry, and that the intensity of what I wanted to write shouldn't be watered down with the distraction of a vocal melody. Because of lockdown restrictions, I had to record all those early vocals into my phone and send them to Marc online. Although he became incredibly proficient at treating the phone recordings, I think you can hear the difference in quality when I was finally able to use a microphone once we were in a position to record in the studio Marc built for us.

I'd definitely do some of those vocals differently now - and not just for technical reasons. Having promised ourselves we'd never play live; in 2022 we asked some talented and trusted musician friends to help us do some gigs. This meant I had to consider how best to convey the pieces - outside of our bubble and in front of actual people. I had to think about persona, and how to bring some physicality to the performance. I've never been one for flinging myself around—I'm not Iggy Pop—but I found that, organically, the prospect of being able to incorporate hand movements, facial expressions and characterisation into a performance affected *what* I was writing, and still does.

However, I'm never going to love performance. The intensity of creation and recording is the incentive for me. The full story of *Unspoken Word* is on our Bandcamp page; but being able to record the vocals live for the first time in the studio led to some incredibly emotional sessions. I definitely allowed myself to become vulnerable; and, again, I wrote with that in mind. We were both in tears as I finished the final vocal.

I thought *Unspoken Word* was our grief album, but you can hear elements of the lingering drudgery and isolation of sadness in *Partially Eaten by Animals*. Through New York's BAGeL Radio, we were lucky enough to make some contacts (dear friends now) in The Netherlands and did some gigs out there. We asked vocalists Joshua Baumgarten of The Irrational Library (*We are The Rudderless*) and Rudie Magieke Kaas of Rick & Rudie (*Underbite*) to contribute vocals and additional lyrics. It was mind-boggling to have such talented and respected company engaging with words that I'd written.

Our new album—*Tough, Listen*—is due out in the latter part of 2024, and as we are still writing for it, it's hard to be objective enough to say how it came about, or what its influences are. It's pretty bleak and industrial, and there's a feeling of alienation throughout; perhaps, in part, a reaction to the result of fourteen years of austerity. People often comment how prolific we are as Dead Anyway; and I guess having released five EPs, six albums and two stand-alone singles in five years (and now, a book!), it could look that way.

But writing words is what I do, as composing music is what Marc does – so what would be the point in waiting around? I'm working on something all the time, although not in a pen-and-paper way: I can't seem to make sense of anything until I've filtered it through words, and then got those words down to my satisfaction on the page.

Writing lyrics, poetry: it's just the way I process the world. Frankly, I dread to think what I'd be without it.

Full Quotes

Kate Arnold, *Kicking at Tombstones*

These 'poems that are also songs' form what might be thought of as a new(ish) genre that I think of as 'grumpy lyricism'. I might also call them Larkin-esque - in that he was the grouchy, miserable, mournful Laureate of a Britain in which the 'nights' are always 'drawing in'. The writer announces at one point that 'there is something wrong with me/I am intravenously off key', and it's a kind of mission statement for the entire collection.

'Grouchy lyricism' might be more accurate; because here we have a 'brillo of ills' and a morning that 'smells of water'. We glimpse 'tights in the gutter', 'tits and teeth' and 'winkle pickers in the curtain'. Odd, unnerving and sour evocations of the contemporary world. So yes, grouchy. But there is also the lyrical, which can be as disarming in its way. So, alongside the 'dead eyeball through the keyhole', we also hear 'lullabies' and see bows tied around the moon. There are 'kisses in whispers' and someone (many poems are directed at various iterations of 'you', and we can only guess at their identities) 'waxed shut my lips with dew'.

Larkin-esque then, but one might also think of other writers who were able to shift between the melancholic and the romantic (perhaps two sides of the same effect). Auden, perhaps. Wilde, perhaps. But these are songs too, so perhaps we might consider Mark E. Smith or certain songs by Joni Mitchell. And one thinks too, perhaps oddly, perhaps surprisingly, of Rap.

But I hear Rap in these poems. These curses, these beefs, these spats. The 'you' the poet speaks to, spits at, disses, especially early on, recalls Rap's attacks and acts of defiance, of boasts and put-downs. 'You' is a 'clever dick' at one point and the poet announces that she also knows 'how to break the receiver' following some other slight or even act of violence. I hear Rap too in the allusions to roadside bouquets, graffiti and the underpass. To roundabouts and skid marks, to blister packs, to feeling 'far too fucking tired'.

Some poems are explicitly Feminist, as they rage against misogyny and impossible body standards, about the tyranny of cosmetic surgery and systemic abuse and terror (Sarah Everard is alluded to). There's Johnson and COVID-19 and Margaret Atwood's famous aphorism about the implicit dangers of masculinity. There's the memorable image of a hung-over father smoking cigarettes while his wife sings Tammy Wynette in the kitchen.

These 'poems that are also songs' are telegrams, with their full stops and their declarations (like Jenny Holzer's later work). They are poems of exhaustion and fury (no surprise that one album title includes the word 'ennui'). They are explicit and allusive, angry with the online banalities of the contemporary world. In a word, 'grumpy.' But also, crucially, the 'you' we become familiar with, in a moment of touching tenderness, 'kissed my tiptoes'. Here we have it: 'the grumpy lyrical'.

Martin Randall - Senior Lecturer Creative Arts University of Gloucestershire

Words can be sartorial too, you know?
Verbal splendour sets certain lyricists apart; as does a sense of mystery, drawing you closer to their work, like a pervy lover of paintings pressing their nose against canvases. It isn't so much what does this mean, as how has this happened?

We get so used to words in songs being used to establish shapes that fit: verse chorus, verse bore us. Not here. Now, Arnold may well be communicating in code to resistance groups. Or we've become party to the middle of a conversation that could kick off a Netflix series, where our heroine returns to her hometown and sets off a tumbling descent into Hell. It is also social commentary, the modern world placed under a microscope, before it gets casually offloaded to the local jumble sale.

All of life is here. What Kate Arnold does, and why Dead Anyway stand out like a lighthouse in a cinema, effectively sends arrows through your usual inertia, evoking memories. Dead Anyway music shifts: no pattern, ablaze with possibilities, reassuringly wild.

These words, pulled from the compost of a furtive, bubbling mind, are flowers with fists.

Mick Mercer - http://www.mickmercer.com

Reading these always makes one think. Later—often days later—a line or two will center itself in one's consciousness and click with a different meaning, or click with a meaning that changes the entire text. And weeks later, that same line may return and shift one's perspective yet again. A rewarding collection which demands repeated explorations.

Ted Leibowitz - BAGeL Radio

www.ingramcontent.com/pod-product-compliance
Lightning Source LLC
Chambersburg PA
CBHW041308110526
44590CB00028B/4291